Practical Wisdom is written
real-world insights will sha... ... ...
avoid the common pitfalls of ministry. Above all, it will stir your
love for Jesus, for His people, and for the calling the Lord has
placed on your life.
—Kel Cunard, Lead Pastor, Good Life Church

I'm thrilled for the work Cody has done in this book. There is
no growth in life and ministry without growing in
wisdom. *Practical Wisdom for Ministry* is a tool you will reach for
often to be taught and reminded of the wisdom principles we all
need to make it the long haul. I'm so thankful for this tool in my
ministry toolbelt.
—Brock Graham, Lead Pastor, Redeemer Bible Church

In this refreshing and easily digestible work, Dr. Podor offers
mature bites of wisdom with self-effacing humility. Putting into
practice each day's expanded proverbial-like content will aid in
establishing solid ministry practices.
**—Brent Aucoin, Ph.D., President of Faith Bible Seminary,
Lafayette, IN**

For anyone engaged in disciple making and praying for wisdom,
Cody has given a gift by collecting some of the most enduring
practical wisdom God has provided in response to his own
prayer. The simple, to-the-point organization of these gems
makes this a book to keep on hand and meditate over frequently.
**—Christian McNeilly, Director of Church Planting, Great
Commission Collective**

Practical Wisdom for Ministry by Pastor Cody Podor provides pithy proverbs for pastoral ministry. As I read this 30-day guide, I thought first of Paul with Timothy. Then another picture came to mind—Timothy with those he was called to disciple. If you are looking for real-world, hands-on, easy-to-digest-and-apply insights for disciplemaking, then this little manual is for you.
—Bob Kellemen, Th.M., Ph.D., Professor of Biblical Counseling Faith Bible Seminary; Author of *Gospel-Centered Counseling: How Christ Changes Lives*

Practical Wisdom For Ministry

A 30-Day Guide For Disciple Makers

CODY PODOR

ISBN: 978-1-7364668-0-3

*To the men and women
that God, in his grace, has used
to help me grow in my love for the Lord.*

CONTENTS

	Introduction	1
1	Quality Over Quantity	5
2	Share The Gospel And Your Life	7
3	God's Spirit, God's Word, And God's People	9
4	Faithfulness Is Greater Than Flashiness	13
5	Pray	15
6	Promise Discretion, Not Confidentiality	17
7	Questions Prick The Conscience	19
8	Stay On Mission	23
9	Time Is Not The Enemy	27
10	Ask Questions First	29
11	I Don't Know. Let Me Think About It.	33
12	Don't Make Disciples Of You	35
13	It's Okay To Speak Up	37
14	It's Okay To Be Quiet	39
15	Old News Is Often New	41
16	Plan Ahead. Work Ahead.	43
17	Look For A. F. T. People	45
18	Clarity And Simplicity	47
19	Don't Try To Be Someone You're Not	49
20	Ask For Feedback	51
21	Communicate	53
22	Rejoice When God Uses Others	55
23	Don't Die On Every Hill	57
24	Read	59
25	Say Hard Things	61

26	Questions To Ask Yourself Regularly	63
27	"Unispeak" Not "Unithink"	65
28	Building Teams	67
29	Take Breaks	69
30	Dependence	71
	Conclusion	73

Notes

INTRODUCTION

"If I have seen further it is by standing on the shoulders of Giants."[1] So penned Isaac Newton in a letter to Robert Hooke in 1675. It's ironic that even this quotation is not originally attributed to Isaac Newton but rather, finds its origination in the 12th century from a man named Bernard of Chartres.

That's what this book is. It's the view that I am experiencing and enjoying as I stand on the shoulders of those who have gone before me. I want to tell you what I see because I believe seeing it will help you serve the Lord with faithfulness, effectiveness, and joy.

Now, there's a lot more that must be said about the intersection of this quote and my life. You see, it begins with "if". That's important. I'm still relatively young and inexperienced. I believe that I have "seen" quite a bit from where I stand now, but I also recognize that I have many more shoulders to climb and my hope is that my vision will only grow clearer. So, this is not a definitive work. This is a work in progress.

When I teach classes, I always begin the first session by stating something like this: We learn what we have been taught and so we teach what we have learned. I do not pretend to be the originator of much, or perhaps anything that you will encounter in this book. If I discuss a matter that is clear, compelling, and helpful, you can be almost certain that I did not come up with it. If there is something that is confusing or curious, that is likely mine.

That's how you should read this little book. Assume that anything profitable is not from me. I will be diligent to give credit to whom it is due, if I am able to remember. However, I am confident that there is much in here that I learned from someone else and has become so ingrained into my thinking that I do not remember from whom I've learned it. Ultimately, if there is wisdom in this book, it comes from God. And so, I would ask that anytime you are helped by these words, you would turn your gaze to the Lord and utter a 'thank you' or a 'praise God'.

Before we begin together, I wanted to make a few notes. First, this work is intended to be practical; not exegetical. I believe that the content I have included is biblical and founded upon solid exegesis of Scripture. But I have not included that work here. Occasionally, I may include a quotation from Scripture or offer a reference. However, the main purpose of this work is not to offer an exegetical defense. Instead, my hope is to offer some practical wisdom that I have gleaned over the years.

Second, each segment is intended to be short. Therefore, I do not contend that I have offered a comprehensive treatment of any one subject. I have offered thirty pieces of wisdom so that you may use this resource over the course of a month. Of course, you may consume the content as quickly as you'd like. But I think taking time to meditate on each of these points may yield a better result in the end.

This may be a perfect resource to offer someone as they are preparing to step onto a ministry team or if they simply want to be better equipped to make disciples. This may be a resource that you return to each year for a refresher course on some (God willing) helpful ideas to consider as you continue in your ministry.

Finally, please know that I am praying for you as you work your way through this resource. I'll conclude by encouraging you to develop a posture of desperate dependence upon the Lord. I want to commend this posture to you even before you begin. In Proverbs 26:7, we are warned, "Like a lame man's legs, which hang useless, is a proverb in the mouth of fools."

1

Quality Over Quantity

I t was my senior year of high school and I had a zeal for
the Lord. I was ready to buy a one-way ticket to Africa
and spend my life for the sake of the gospel. No
college. No more preparation. Just me, my Bible, my
youthful arrogance, and my vain idealism. What more does
one need when trying to singlehandedly rescue the world?

I remember Kel, the man whom the Lord used to
disciple me during this season, inviting me out for lunch. As
we sat in the back of his truck, he patiently listened to me
wax eloquently about all my future ministry plans. After a
remarkably kind period of silent listening, he asked one
simple question, "Cody, have you thought about what it
would look like to have a quality of years in ministry rather
than a quantity of years in ministry?" No explanation. No
pleading with me to reconsider. Just one simple question
that changed the trajectory of my life.

Zeal is a beautiful thing. When coupled with arrogance
and idealism, it can be a mighty dangerous thing. As you
consider a lifetime of serving the Lord, can I ask you to
consider the same question? What would it look like for you

to have a quality of years in ministry rather than a quantity? For me, it meant coupling the active work of ministry with the pursuit of further education. It meant a quieter, more hidden, seemingly less heroic kind of service. It meant many hours by myself reading and writing. It meant submitting to teachers, more mature brothers and sisters, and other ministry leaders.

If you are chomping at the bit to get to the 'real work of the ministry', praise God for your passion. Now, enroll in the school of slow Christian maturity and do the hard, quiet work of growing in your love and knowledge of the Lord so that you can serve faithfully and effectively by God's grace.

2

Share The Gospel And Your Life

When I ask a lot of people starting out in ministry what gets them most excited about serving the Lord, many respond by discussing how excited they are to teach the Word. Don't get me wrong, teaching the Word of God is a glorious opportunity. But it's not everything in ministry. Perhaps you've heard the adage, "people don't care how much you know until they know how much you care." It's true.

In 1 Thessalonians 2:8 Paul says, "So, being affectionately desirous of you, we were ready to share with you not only the gospel of God but also our own selves, because you had become very dear to us." I remember the first time a man who discipled me spoke about this passage. He said this was his ministry verse and since that day, it has become my ministry verse as well. It is an intriguing passage. Here is the Apostle Paul saying that he wanted to share more than just the gospel with the people that he was ministering to. Yes, he majored on the gospel. His life was spent for the advancement of the good news of Jesus Christ. But he wasn't just some sage on the stage. He didn't come into town simply to do his next speaking gig. Paul wanted to share the gospel and his life with people.

What does it look like to share your life with others? It requires a lot of time, a lot of listening, and a lot of heartache. To genuinely share your life with others, you have to *be* with others. You have to make the time for meals and activities. You have to enter into their passions. Listen to their stories and struggles. Make yourself available. You also have to be transparent, sharing your story and your struggles.

What compels your desire to proclaim the gospel and teach others the Word of God? Is it genuine love for God and others? Or is it something else? Genuine love will lead to a ministry that is characterized not only by faithful proclamation of truth but also faithful sharing of your life.

3

God's Spirit, God's Word, And God's People

God's Spirit, God's Word, and God's people. These are the three essential ingredients for making disciples. After an individual understands and embraces the gospel, it will be by these three gifts from God that the individual will make any progress in the Christian life.

The Bible teaches us that hundreds of things happen to us when we turn from our sins and trust in Jesus. Included in this list is the indwelling presence of the Holy Spirit. Spiritual growth will only happen by the power of the Spirit at work in the believer. Therefore, it is always crucial to discern the genuineness of someone's relationship with the Lord when they are seeking to grow in Christ-likeness. Without the Spirit, the individual will not advance. This is why Paul rebukes the Galatians in Galatians 3:3, "Are you so foolish? Having begun by the Spirit, are you now being perfected by the flesh?"

The Spirit of God uses the Word of God to bring about transformation. In Romans 12:2, Paul exhorts, "Do not be conformed to this world, but be transformed by the renewal of your mind..." Again, in Ephesians 4:22–23 he says, "to put off your old self, which belongs to your former manner of life and is corrupt through deceitful desires, and to be renewed in the spirit of your minds, and to put on the new self, created after the likeness of God in true righteousness and holiness." If we want to change, then it will begin in the life of the mind. As the Spirit helps us to think God's thoughts, our desires change. People do what they do, because they want what they want (James 4:1–2). People want what they want, because they think what they think. If we are to grow—and help others to grow—then we must meditate on the truth and so be changed by it. The renewing of our minds doesn't just happen by virtue of reading words on a page. The bridge between information and transformation is meditation. We will only grow in Christ as the Spirit of God changes us by the Word of God.

Finally, we must realize that God has not just called us to himself in Christ. He has also called us to one another. The Christian life is a team sport; not an individual sport. We need each other. God designed it this way. This is why there are more than 50 Scriptural commands to care for one another. This is why we are encouraged stir one another up to love and good works, not forsaking meeting together (Hebrews 10:24–25). This is why the writer of Hebrews encourages us in Hebrews 3:12–14, "Take care, brothers, lest there be in any of you an evil, unbelieving heart, leading you to fall away from the living God. But exhort one another every day, as long as it is called 'today,' that none of you may be hardened by the deceitfulness of sin. For we have come to share in Christ, if indeed we hold our original confidence firm to the end."

If you are going to grow in your relationship with the

Lord and if you are going to help others grow in their relationships with the Lord, it will only be by the Spirit of God at work through the Word of God and the People of God. So, encourage those you are discipling to cry out for the active working of the Spirit in their lives. Encourage them to meditate on truth from God's Word. And encourage them to be connected to a local church.

4

Faithfulness Is Greater Than Flashiness

We are not laboring to make fans. We are laboring to make disciples. Fans are fickle. Perhaps you have heard it said, "you keep people with whatever you attracted them with." Constantly trying to do the next big thing or keep up with the current trend is exhausting. Often in ministry, you shouldn't be seeking to do something new. You should strive for faithfulness.

Stop and consider the individuals who have had the greatest impact on your life. What stands out about these people? My guess is that a lot of ordinary moments come to mind. That person was there for you when you faced a difficult circumstance. Every time you saw that individual interact with their spouse, it was full of grace and love. Perhaps that person was part of your life for an extended season. It's likely that the people who have had the greatest impact on your life have not done anything particularly spectacular. They have just been a faithful presence in your life and have consistently demonstrated what it looks like to fear God and follow Jesus.

If you're responsible for leading a ministry, don't get caught up in what this church or that church is doing. Yes, be aware. And absolutely be willing to try something new. But don't get caught up in constantly pivoting your ministry. Find some solid people that love the Lord and love others and get these people together to worship the Lord, to pray together, and to learn from his Word. Do it with excellence. But don't get distracted with all the flashy new ideas. By God's grace, just be faithful.

5

Pray

I am a proud man. I have an over-inflated view of myself and my abilities. I have a tendency to be generous with myself and strict with others. I often forget John the Baptizer's word in John 3:27, "A person cannot receive even one thing unless it is given him from heaven." I lose sight of the fact that the work I am trying to accomplish in ministry is spiritual work and so requires spiritual weapons. I value efficiency too highly. I am impatient. I put too much stock in what can be accomplished by man.

And so, I don't pray. Not near as much as I ought to. By God's grace, don't be like me.

6

Promise Discretion, Not Confidentiality

L et's say you promise confidentiality to a student who then feels comfortable to share with you about the abuse he is suffering at the hands of his parents. Now what? By law, you must report the abuse. But you promised confidentiality. You're compromised. There is no question as to the mandatory nature of reporting the abuse. So, you have to look that student in the eyes and say, "I know I promised confidentiality, but I have no choice. I have to tell the authorities."

Instead of promising confidentiality, make the promise of discretion. At the beginning of these kinds of conversations, I tell people that I take it very seriously that they would be willing to share a burden with me. I assure them that I will steward the information well. And then, I tell them that I will only share what I must with whom I must when I must. It's the promise of discretion.

The promise says that I am not going to repeat everything they tell me. I will only communicate the information that I absolutely must share with others. The promise says that I am not going to take this information and share it with lots of people. I will only share with people who need to know in order to be a help in the situation. And finally, the promise says that I will not share information with others until it becomes necessary to share.

When providing a forum for people to share their hurts with you, you cannot offer confidentiality because you have no idea what they are about to share. Instead, promise them discretion and then, be faithful to your promise.

7

Questions Prick The Conscience

Here's the easy way to deal with conflict: make a record of wrongs and then set up a time to meet with that person to read your list of grievances from top to bottom never granting the other person an opportunity to speak. Then, get out of there as quickly as possible.

Like I said, it's the easy way but it's also the most ineffective and harmful way to deal with conflict. Handling conflict in this way violates 1 Corinthians 13, where we are commanded to not keep a record of wrongs. It also violates James 1:19, where we are exhorted to be slow to speak and quick to listen. So, how do we handle confrontation in a way that honors God and loves the person we are confronting? Remember this: questions prick the conscience but accusations stir up wrath.

Most people do not enjoy confrontation. It's uncomfortable. The people we confront rarely respond well in the moment. We fear what may result after the confrontation. It's easier to ignore issues or just look for some other way to deal with them.

Have you noticed that you're a sinner? And did you ever notice that sin has a way of blinding you to the truth? I know I sure have. Sin has a way of distorting the facts and making it difficult for us to discern what's really going on in our lives and what is really going on in our hearts. This is true of every single individual that we interact with. So, if we are going to help others grow in the Lord, it's going to require confrontation. We are going to have to speak the truth into their lives when they have been blinded by their sin or when they justify themselves in their sin.

When you believe that confrontation is the next right thing to do, come up with a list of questions rather than a list of accusations. Request a time to meet and enter into that conversation as a learner; not an interrogator. Begin by asking how the other person is doing and genuinely care about his response. And then, ask a lot more questions. Can you share with me what happened? What was going on in your thinking when you did that? What were you wanting? How do you think that made others feel? Do you think that was the right thing to do? If you could go back and change it, would you have done anything differently? What passages of Scripture did you consider when you made that choice? Did you talk to anyone else before you made that decision? The list could go on.

Asking questions is the most effective tool you have when it comes to confrontation. When people make decisions, it's likely that they have not thought through every question you will ask. If they have, it is almost certain that they have not articulated those responses out loud for their own ears to hear. By asking questions, you are helping the other individual process his thinking and offering him the opportunity to evaluate his actions.

Asking questions is not expedient. It takes a lot more time than lodging accusations. Asking questions doesn't feed the fleshly desire to tell someone off. Asking questions demonstrates humility. You don't enter into the confrontation as the omniscient judge who has come to bring revelation. Perhaps you will learn that the other individual was right in what he did and the need for confrontation doesn't exist. Perhaps the individual you are confronting will begin to see clearly throughout your conversation and be drawn to repentance without you having to explicitly call him to repentance. Perhaps it will soften his heart to hear you when you do have to explicitly tell him his sin and encourage him to repent.

8

Stay On Mission

I like our church's mission statement: we exist to glorify God and make disciples. It's simple and it's biblical. It prioritizes doxology—giving glory to God—while being mindful of soteriology—making disciples. Why is this so important? Because one of the most prolific conversations you will have as a leader is with people who are passionate about all kinds of things that are not in line with the mission. And praise God for their passion. Just be careful that other people's passions do not diminish the mission.

I was taught to think about how effective every opportunity would be at advancing the mission. If the opportunity was dead center of our mission, it would be like advancing ten steps down the path of accomplishing our goal. If it contributed in only a small manner to the accomplishing of the mission, it would be like advancing one step down the path. Once you determine how many steps an opportunity will take you towards advancing your mission, then allocate a direct proportion of resources towards that opportunity. These resources include: time, money, people, thought, and energy.

Another helpful concept is to determine if the opportunity you are considering is our-thing, your-thing, or not-our-thing. If an opportunity is our-thing, then it aligns with our mission and directly advances what we are trying to do as a ministry. If it is your-thing, then it is a God-glorifying opportunity but it is not necessarily in line with our specific mission. If it is not-our-thing, it is either unhelpful or so far off mission that we don't want to invest any thought or time in the opportunity. Here is an example of each in my ministry setting:

Our Thing

Each year, we host a retreat for our high school students. This is our thing and this is a ten-step opportunity. It directly fulfills the mission of glorifying God and making disciples. Because this is our thing and it is a ten-step opportunity, we will communicate to our church family about it and allocate significant resources to execute the retreat with excellence.

Your Thing

Some students approached me about doing a Bible drive. They wanted to put out a box in the back of the meeting room and have the opportunity announced from the front. This is a your-thing opportunity. Bible drives are great. Students passionate about collecting Bibles for those who do not have them is a good thing. But, it is not our thing as a ministry. I want to encourage these students and help them think about how they can engage others in this opportunity, but I would not announce it from the front and allow them to put a collection box in the back of our meeting room. Sounds pretty harsh, right? In our ministry, we have almost 200 students. Most of them have opportunities that they are passionate about. And they are God-glorifying opportunities. If we announced every one of the opportunities and put collection boxes in the back for each of them, all we would do is make announcements and there would be no room to meet because the room would be full of boxes. Perhaps this is a bit of an exaggeration but I hope you're following me.

Not Our Thing

Finally, there are the not-our-thing opportunities. These might be opportunities that would be counterproductive or harmful to the mission. These might be opportunities that you would want to shepherd your people away from.

There is a lot of good that can be done. Be careful that you stay on mission when it comes to the good you decide to do. And thoughtfully consider how you can spur on those who are doing other good work in other places.

9

Time Is Not The Enemy

ave I mentioned that I value efficiency? I also appreciate expediency. Honestly, who doesn't? When we want something, we want it now. Tom Petty was right, "the waiting is the hardest part." And yet, the Christian life is one of slow progress. I think this is one reason why many of the biblical writers chose the word "walk" to describe the Christian life.

Think about Noah. It took him around 100 years to build the ark. That's 36,500 days of trusting the Lord, chopping down tress, and piecing together a massive boat. Consider Abraham. He was 75 years old when the Lord promised him a son. Isaac isn't born until Abraham is 100 years old. That's a 25-year-old promise. That's 25 years of waiting on the Lord. That's 25 years of God shaping Abraham through the daily discipline of waiting. Finally, consider Jesus. God makes a promise to Adam and Eve in Genesis 3 and then orchestrates centuries of redemptive history before the coming of Christ.

Time is not the enemy. Rome wasn't built in a day. And on, and on the sayings go. Transformation occurs over time.

Spending your life to see others grow and mature in Christ will take time. Don't get so caught up in looking for growth this week, this month, or even this year. Don't expect that a weekend retreat or conference is suddenly going to bring about a seismic shift in people's lives. Don't anticipate a sermon or teaching time to initiate revival. Keep the long-view when it comes to serving others and seeking their growth. It doesn't happen all at once and it often occurs through incremental, indiscernible changes over a period of time. If you have to chop down a tree every time you pick up an axe, you will only try to take down small trees.[2] Big, beautiful trees that can be made into something great take a thousand strikes. Some plant, some water, but God gives the growth. Trust the Lord and be faithful to plant and water.

10

Ask Questions First

Proverbs 18:2, "A fool takes no pleasure in understanding, but only in expressing his opinion." This one verse changed more than 95% of my conversations. The reality is, most of us think we are pretty great and that people should hear what we have to say. We love it when people come to us and seek our advice. We love to be the answer-guy. It scratches that itch for feeling important and needed. But how often do we breeze past really understanding a situation before we begin to speak into it?

One of the most important tools in the toolbox for relationships is the art of question asking. God tells us that we are acting foolishly if we don't take the time to really understand a situation that is going on in people's lives. We may offer them bad counsel, irrelevant counsel, or simply steer them in a good direction rather than the best direction.

Now, here's the problem: asking questions means that I have to invest more time and more energy into the person. Rather than just dispensing knowledge like a gumball machine or writing a prescription to quickly cover up the symptoms, we should take the time to understand what's going on under the surface. This will take time. This will require active listening. This will force us to think. But it will be so very worth it.

Not only will asking questions help us respond better, but it will also enlarge the influence that we have in people's lives. Asking questions and listening well to others demonstrates a level of love and care. As people sense your love for them as you offer them the gift of time and listening, they will receive your counsel with a greater readiness to respond to it appropriately.

Here are some types of questions you may consider asking:

Discovery Questions

These are questions that help you learn more about the situation. Who was involved? Has this happened before? How often do you deal with this? Do you experience these same issues in other relationships? How long has this been going on?

Motive Questions

These are questions that seek to uncover the person's heart. What were you wanting? Why do you think you said that? If you could wave a magic wand and have your perfect scenario, what would it look like?

Follow-Up Questions

These are questions that help you gather important details. Can you tell me more about that? What were you thinking and feeling when that happened? Why do you think you reacted that way? How can you avoid that in the future? What do you think we need to do next?

Survey Questions

These are great for drawing out meaningful dialogue. On a scale from 1–10, rate your walk with God, your marriage, your relationship with _____, your struggle with _____. Once they give you a response, ask why they selected that number. Then, ask what it would look like to be at a healthier number.

Seek to understand a situation before you speak into it. This is one of the biblical truths that relieves us from feeling like we have to fix every situation the instant someone shares it with us. I often respond to others by saying, "Thank you so much for sharing that with me. I would really like to learn more about it before I respond. Could we set up a time to discuss this further?"

11

I Don't Know. Let Me Think About It.

Sometimes in discipleship, it feels like you have to know all the answers. After all, people are looking to you to guide them. Often, you are one of the first people they will come to with a question that they have been thinking about for a while. But just because they have been thinking about it for a while doesn't mean that you have. This is the right time to say, "hmm, that's an interesting question. I don't know, but let me think about it and get back to you."

Release yourself from the pressure of thinking that you have to be the expert on everything. People find it refreshing when they hear that you don't know everything and they feel well loved when you tell them that you will take some of your time to think deeply about what matters to them. Just make sure you follow through by putting some thought into their question and initiating the conversation before too long.

12

Don't Make Disciples Of You

I was standing in another pastor's office expressing frustration over some decisions that another person in our church family was making. This other pastor listened patiently, asked me some questions, and challenged me by saying, "It sounds like you are upset because they are not making the decisions you would have made. But do you think their decisions are sinful?" As we continued to discuss, it became apparent that I lost sight of shepherding people toward becoming more like Jesus and instead, I was trying to make people like me.

God created all of us uniquely. A quick survey of all the strengths finders and personality-type models demonstrates that we all share this understanding. The goal is not to make people more like me by caring about what I care about, having the same strengths, pursuing the same goals, or sharing my same passions. Discipleship is about helping people become more like Jesus while retaining the uniqueness of who God created them to be. We need to be careful that we don't try to fit people into our mold.

Of course, Paul does say "Be imitators of me, as I am of Christ" in 1 Corinthians 11:1. People should be able to look at and imitate our conduct, our teaching, our faithfulness, and our aim in life. We should seek to be an example of godliness to others in our lives. But, we must always remember that we are called to make disciples of Christ; not of ourselves.

13

It's Okay To Speak Up

Length of time + solid relationships = credit to speak up. If it's your first week on the job or if the relationship is brand new, it may not be the wisest time to speak up. But if you have been around long enough to be a learner and you have invested in relationships such that people know your love for the Lord and for them, then you have gained the platform to speak up. Deference is good but likely, so are your thoughts. Not every hill is worth dying on but some hills definitely are. So, when given the opportunity to be a part of a dialogue or a decision-making process, don't be afraid to open your mouth and offer your thoughts.

14

It's Okay To Be Quiet

In Proverbs 17:28, God's Word says, "Even a fool who keeps silent is considered wise; when he closes his lips, he is deemed intelligent." You don't have to speak into everything. Quietness does not inherently signify weakness or ignorance. Perhaps you know that person who is often quiet while others carry on the conversation. It could be hours before she opens her mouth. But the moment she does, everyone stops. Everyone listens. They know that when she speaks, she really has something to say and they had better listen up.

Some people employ the strategy of throwing as much against the wall as possible and seeing what sticks. Others only put something out there when they deem it absolutely necessary and helpful. Don't feel like you always have to be a leading contributor in terms of quantity. Think about offering a quality contribution that will gain a better hearing. And remember, not every hill is worth dying on. Seriously.

15

Old News Is Often New

If you have been submerged in the Christian subculture for a long time, you often hear the same phrases used again and again. Language is a building block of culture. Shared language that is often repeated is powerful in cultivating and maintaining culture.

I spent 12 years pastoring in student discipleship. There would be times in conversations or in teaching when I would hesitate to say a certain phrase because I felt like it was cliché or tired. But, what I came to realize is that cliché phrases are cliché for a reason. Many of them succinctly communicate an important truth that is worth repeating. And think about the first time you heard something like "sin always over-promises but under-delivers." It's profound. It's memorable. It preaches. And it likely has come into your mind when battling sin.

We don't necessarily need to be creative with our content. We need to be faithful.

16

Plan Ahead. Work Ahead.

K now what you have to do tomorrow before today is over. Before I leave my office for the day, I spend some time writing down all the items that I need to accomplish the next day. So, when I arrive in the morning—the most productive part of my day and the part of my day when I do my best work—I don't have to waste my energy thinking about what needs to be done. I can get right to work and maximize these precious hours.

Working ahead is also critical. If you procrastinate, then you force yourself into a corner. The deadline is approaching and you have to meet it. No matter what. This removes the possibility of having margin in your life to love others well. If you are always racing against the clock, then you won't have time for something to come up. You will be forced to sacrifice something.

Plan ahead. Work ahead. This will help you love and serve well.

17

Look for A. F. T. People

Available. Faithful. Teachable. These are three qualities that you should look for when seeking to disciple and equip others. Of course, there are plenty of other traits that come to mind when considering what kind of person you want to invest in. But without these three, it will be difficult to gain much ground.

I put available first on purpose. If the person you are attempting to pour into is too busy or can only offer a little time to you on occasion, it is likely that you won't gain much ground in discipleship. This is a challenge because people with competency and experience are sought after. Their opportunities abound and so they may already be engaged in too much activity. Don't frustrate yourself by trying to grasp for any moment you can get with them. Instead, look for someone who is available even if they need more development.

The people you seek to invest in need to be faithful. This goes beyond the mere availability of time. They need to be dependable and committed. As we said earlier in #9, it takes a significant amount of time to see transformation in people's lives. If they are not committed to making the necessary time and demonstrating that commitment by faithfully showing up, they are not the kind of people that you want to invest your efforts in when it comes to development.

Finally, look for teachable people. A teachable person is different from a 'yes person'. Questions and challenges from others do not render them unteachable. What is their disposition when they question you? Is their question genuine or is it argumentative? Are they willing to change their position throughout the dialogue? Are they more interested in teaching or in learning?

The word 'aft' is a nautical term that denotes the rear of a watercraft. A. F. T. people, that is—people who are available, faithful, and teachable—are the kind of servant leaders who are willing to sit in the back while they develop. They also recognize that in every season of life, no matter how experienced or knowledgeable, there is a need to sit in the back again and keep learning.

18

Clarity and Simplicity

Your people need clarity and simplicity. They don't need you to sound smart. They need to understand you. They don't need to think that you're the expert because of how complex everything must be. They need you to offer a simple way forward in complex matters. Remember, the goal in loving and leading others is not to make them more dependent on you. The goal is to work yourself out of the job and set them up to live faithfully long after you're gone.

It's easy to hide behind ambiguous communication. In the Broadway show *Hamilton*, Aaron Burr meets Alexander Hamilton. During their initial introduction, Burr encourages Hamilton not to run his mouth and to never let people know what he is against or for. Hamilton later responds, "If you stand for nothing Burr, what'll you fall for?" This doesn't mean that you have to make a statement about everything. But, when you do say something, make sure you actually say something. Be clear about where you stand and know why you stand there.

When it comes to simplicity, we need to recognize that most things in life are not all that complicated. They may be hard but that doesn't make them complicated. Being able to simplify information or strategy to make it accessible to the masses is one of the greatest gifts a leader can offer his people. While oversimplification is a real danger, people more often fall into the error of overcomplicating matters.

19

Don't Try To Be Someone You're Not

Praise God for faithful, more mature, more experienced believers. Every disciple maker should have men or women who are further down the road than they are to look up to and to follow their way of life. But be careful that you don't try to become the people that you admire.

Remember, God made you uniquely and he did that on purpose. Don't spend precious time and energy on trying to become someone you were never created to be. Think about the disciples. Peter was Peter. Jesus never expected him to be like John. He expected Peter to grow in godliness while remaining Peter.

This is part of what Paul is communicating in 1 Corinthians when he tells the saints in Corinth to stop exalting any one apostle. Paul, Apollos, and Cephas were all different and each was used by God in a unique way to be a blessing to the church. Unity is important, but it's very different from uniformity. The Word teaches us that we are all like different members of the body that come together to create something that is more valuable than the sum of its parts. Ears shouldn't seek to be hands and hands shouldn't seek to be mouths.

So yes, examine the lives of those you admire in the faith. Emulate the godliness that you perceive. But don't try to replicate those individuals. It will be forced and awkward. Instead, pursue holiness and ask that the Lord would work through the way he made you to be a blessing to others.

20

Ask For Feedback

You work hard to prepare. You spend time praying to make sure your heart is right. And then, you deliver the sermon, teach the class, meet with the individual, or have the really difficult conversation. Then, you breathe a deep sigh of relief and move on. Mission accomplished. What's next?

There's just one important step you missed. Asking for feedback. Now, this isn't a fishing for compliments escapade. This isn't seeking out those who gush over you and the gifts that God has given you. Asking for feedback is an opportunity to hear from others how they perceive you are doing. Of course, you want encouragement. But, it's also helpful to receive constructive criticism.

Some of us are self-aware. Most of us struggle at introspection. We need to humble ourselves to those around us who love us and who would be willing to speak truth into our lives so that we can continue to grow in our ability to serve effectively. Don't passively wait for people to share with you. Instead, be proactive. Before you teach, ask a few people if they would listen with an analytical ear. Set up a time to hear from them. If you're having a difficult conversation and a third-party is present, take some time to debrief.

Pride knows. Humility listens. Ask people for honest, real feedback. And when they do share, receive their insights graciously and thoughtfully. If you respond with a defensive spirit, you will likely burn that avenue for feedback in the future.

21

Communicate

Communication is one of the most important skills in building relationships and in leading others. I've heard it said that leaders must aim to be clear and expect to be misunderstood.[3] When we communicate, we need to do so early, often, and in many ways.

Communicate Early

This requires forethought and diligent planning. If we are always working on projects at the last minute, then we won't have anything to communicate until the last minute. If we work ahead, then we will have plenty of time to consider who needs to know what and how early they need to know it. When we communicate early, we demonstrate to others that we respect their time and recognize that they have other responsibilities in life.

Communicate Often

It takes multiple communications to transmit a message. If you think that people ought to hear you, understand you, and plan accordingly after your initial communication, then you will set yourself up for a whole lot of frustration. This is connected to the learning process. When people learn something new, they begin with exposure. This is the initial introduction. Once they hear it again, exposure gives way to familiarity. As time goes on, and people continue to hear the same message, familiarity becomes understanding.

Communicate in Many Ways

Some people are visual. Some are auditory. Some need to read in order to understand. If you have an important message, you need to communicate it through several mediums. Follow an email up with a brief mention when you're gathered in-person. Create a video to reinforce whatever you just wrote. Communicate to the masses and then follow up with one-on-one conversations.

Communication is critical in developing relationships and leading others. So, when you communicate, communicate early, often, and in many ways.

22

Rejoice When God Uses Others

Jealousy is icky. Being the jealous person feels awful. Seeing a jealous person is entirely unattractive. This is particularly true when it comes to seeing the Lord at work through other people. What is your desire for those you love and lead? Is it to see them grow in Christ? Or, is it to see them grow in Christ specifically through your ministry?

When we see the Lord working in people's lives that we love, it should matter very little who the Lord is using to bring about the growth. There will be seasons where the Lord will grant you a certain level of influence in another individual's life, but that does not mean you will have that influence forever. Be quick to champion God's work in your people's lives no matter where it is coming from. Be quick to cheer on other leaders in your ministry. Be quick to rejoice when God uses others to build up the church. After all, it's not about you. It's about him.

23

Don't Die On Every Hill

This has been notoriously difficult for me. I am wired in such a way where I see the world as black and white. I am quick to elevate matters to a question of principle or morality rather than to see them as preferential. And, I am passionate. When I care about something, I really care a lot about it. The confluence of these realities often turns situations into a matter of life or death for me. Here's the problem though: if you are willing to die on every hill, it's likely that you're going to do a lot of dying.

There are matters of great significance. When we rightly discern a situation and determine that it is, in fact, of much import, then we ought to be willing to stand for what we believe. But not every issue rises to this level. It can be very difficult for everyone involved when every issue is elevated to "I'm willing to die for my position."

This means that you will have to make choices. One of my professors in seminary made this jarring observation: there is sin in every camp, you just need to determine which kinds of sin you can live with. To be clear, he was not condoning sin in any way. Rather, he was making the point that there will always be different preferences or issues in your circumstances. There are some that you have to live with. Let's face it, nothing in life is 'have it your way' other than Burger King. In every setting you find yourself in, you will have to learn to coexist with people or preferences that you wouldn't have chosen if you were the unilateral decision maker.

So, don't die on every hill. But do discern which hills are worth dying on. And on those, fight valiantly with meekness.

24

Read

In almost every book on leadership or personal development, there is a section dedicated to the importance of reading. The life of the mind is critical to healthy and effective discipleship. Reading provides an avenue for extended meditation. It allows you to get into someone else's head and to listen to their thoughts all the while evaluating their thoughts and perhaps beginning to synthesize them into your life.

Life is busy. Leaders are constantly bombarded with tasks and conversations. If you don't intentionally make time to read, it won't happen. And if you don't guard your time to read, it will certainly be stripped away by some urgent and pressing matter. This is when it becomes so important to remember why you read. It has the potential to make you a healthier and more effective disciple maker.

I know some that read broadly. This gives them an introduction to lots of different thoughts and helps them to have a greater grasp on various fields of thought. Just remember what Charles Spurgeon said of hasty reading,

"Little learning and much pride come of hasty reading."[4] So read broadly, but be careful.

I know of others that have a list of five to ten books that they read through each year. Rather than reading everything new under the sun, they have found books that have so shaped their thinking that they need to return to these books often. If, in their reading outside of this rotation, they find another book that has a profound impact, they remove a book from the list and substitute it with the new one.

The point is, commit yourself to reading. There are many ways you may go about this endeavor but do be diligent to make the time for it and have a plan. Leaders are readers. Leaders are learners.

25

Say Hard Things

In Proverbs 27:6 we read, "Faithful are the wounds of a friend." In Ephesians 4:15, Paul exhorts God's people to speak the truth in love. And sometimes, the truth is not pretty. If we are to really love and lead people well, we will need to say some hard things sometimes. To lovingly communicate a sin pattern that you see in someone's life is not cruel, it is kindness. While the nature of the conversation may be confrontational, it is nevertheless loving.

Please remember #7, questions prick the conscience but accusations stir up wrath. Just because you may have to say hard things from time to time, it doesn't mean that you should do so without any consideration or tact.

I fear, however, that too often people would rather say nothing at all than to speak a difficult truth to someone. If we are not faithful to lovingly communicate other's errors, how will they grow? How will relationships be reconciled? How will things change that desperately need to change? How will we avoid finding ourselves in this same sad scenario a few weeks down the road?

God says some hard things in the Bible. Jesus said some really hard things during his earthly ministry. Paul said some hard things to Peter that we read about in the book of Galatians. And Scripture often encourages us to say hard things to one another so that we may grow up in every way and build up the body of Christ in love.

26

Questions To Ask Yourself Regularly

For years, I have used these three questions to evaluate my heart and to lead me in praying before I proclaim the Word of God. I believe these questions apply outside of just preparing to preach. I try to ask myself these questions regularly:

1. Am I worried about what people think or what God thinks?

2. Do I genuinely love these people?

3. Am I depending on the Spirit's power or my own?

I want to be bold, loving, and dependent upon the Lord. By regularly asking myself these questions, I am constantly evaluating my progress in each of these areas. As I answer honestly, I can better direct my praying and ask for the Lord's help.

27

"Unispeak" Not "Unithink"

God, in his sovereignty, has created you in a unique fashion and has placed you in the position that you hold. When you're working on a team, it's important that you take this into account as you consider your contribution. It can be dangerous if everyone at the table thinks in the exact same way. A hard-fought-for unity is better than a frictionless unity.

It's healthy and okay for God's people to disagree. We ought to critically evaluate options, analyze decisions, offer differing points of view, create thoughtful arguments for our positions, present them in a persuasive manner, and then, have a spirit of humility that graciously accepts the consensus of the room.

If we all think in the same way ("unithink"), then we will proceed with blind spots. We will fail to consider every possible option. We will get stuck in our thinking and lack creativity. And worse, if we think differently but are unwilling to share our thoughts, then the team does not benefit from the way that God has created us. Fear, insecurity, laziness, the desire to be liked—these are all reasons that may keep us from speaking up. By God's grace, we must overcome these sinful deterrents and allow the Lord to use our perspective how he sees fit.

"Unispeak" is just as critical. After you have sat around the table as a team and each person has contributed their unique perspective, decisions must be made. Once a decision is made by the team, the whole team should own the decision. It would be damaging to say, "Well, that's where we ultimately landed but I think it is a horrible idea." This undermines the authority of the whole, fosters a culture of distrust, and ultimately leads to dissension. When you're on a team, do the hard work of disagreeing and offering different perspectives. And then, only after you have done this work, make a decision and own it as a unified whole.

28

Building Teams

B uilding teams may be one of the most important tasks you do as a leader. Building the right team will have a significant impact on the effectiveness of work and the joy that you experience in the work. It's been said, "If you want to go fast, go alone. If you want to go far, bring a team." We all know that it is often easier and more expedient to do something alone. After all, you don't need to ask for input, you don't need to check-in on how others are doing, and you're able to adapt quickly to changes in the scenario. But going alone rarely produces the best result and always misses an opportunity to pour into others and seek their growth.

As disciple makers, we should constantly be seeking opportunities to develop those around us. Every team should have members on it with varying levels of competency and experience. At first, you may need to invite people on the team that are more competent and more experienced. But over time, as you consider helping others grow, you should look to bring people of promise onto your teams.

If you bring someone onto the team that you intend to develop, then you need to have a plan to develop that individual. I have seen too many people placed into positions where they were not given the tools they needed for success. Building teams is not just about finding the right people. It also includes shaping the right people.

It's just as important to ask people to step off your team when it's not going well. Keeping an individual on your team who is unable to perform the functions of his role can be toxic. Of course, you want to be patient with people and allow them space to grow. If the person is not inherently problematic to the team, then look for another role on the team that he can fulfill. But if the person in question continues to lack in his ability to perform, then it may be time to thank him for his work and lovingly direct him to another opportunity. Failure to do this can be a de-motivator to the rest of the team. I think sometimes, we get so focused on trying to care for the struggling individual that we lose sight of the whole. Sometimes, out of fear of hurting the struggling individual, we fail to have hard conversations. Over time, the hurt comes either way.

Look for the right people. Shape the right people. Let the wrong people go. You'll have to do all three if you are going to build effective teams.

29

Take Breaks

There has never been a shortage of opportunities to do good. There are infinite ways that we can serve the Lord and be a blessing to others. It would be entirely possible to spend 168 hours every week in the service of others. And yet, you know your finitude. You grow tired. You feel rundown. Your exhaustion produces a lack of motivation. Joy fades in ceaseless striving.

If you're reading this, it's likely that you genuinely have a heart to love and serve others. Often, it can be difficult to cease from laboring. But you must. Rest is a necessity if you are going to faithfully serve the Lord and others for your whole life. If you do not build a rhythm of rest into your life, then you will not make it.

Rest daily. At 4PM, I close my computer, get up from my desk, and head out of the office for the day. This doesn't mean I am done loving and serving others for the day. I head home to love and serve my family. But, there is a clear ceasing from my office work. The work is never done at 4PM. You must choose to stop.

Rest weekly. I take Mondays off. This has worked well for me as my role requires long hours on Sundays. It is a day built into the week that I can count on to be with family and away from the office. My whole family looks forward to Mondays. It is a day to be together. A day to slow down. A day to do something fun or to do nothing at all.

Rest annually. I personally do not like the word 'vacation'. The whole concept of the word is about vacating your responsibilities. I don't think this is a Christian conception of rest. While it is not a word we use often in the U.S., I prefer the word 'holiday' or 'holy-day'. The idea is a set apart time that is different from the rest of life. You are not vacating your responsibilities when you go on holiday. You are recognizing your weakness and your need to recharge. You are acknowledging the reality that rest is required if you are to continue to have the energy to love and serve faithfully.

30

Dependence

The Christian life is dependence. Of course, all of life is dependence upon the Lord. He is the One who gives life and breath to all mankind. But a theme that we see all through Scripture is the Christian's dependence upon the Lord for anything that is pleasing to God. We are dependent upon the Lord to give us spiritual life when we are spiritually dead. We are dependent upon the Lord to remove our heart of stone and replace it with a heart of flesh. We are dependent upon the Lord to will and to work for his good pleasure. We are dependent upon the Lord for any progress that we experience in our sanctification. We are dependent upon the Lord to cause us to persevere in the faith. We are dependent upon the Lord for everything.

Simply put, Jesus says in John 15:5, "Apart from me, you can do nothing." Dear friend, discipleship is supernatural work. Ultimately, our desire is to see people transformed in their inner being. This is not work that we can do. No matter your skill, experience, or capacity, you cannot effect supernatural change. If you do one thing well in your life and ministry, do this—depend upon the Lord in all things.

This will rightly put you in a place of humility and this will exalt the glorious power of God.

CONCLUSION

I hope this concise resource has helped you experience the view that I have been enjoying as I stand on the shoulders of those who have gone before me. I hope that it has been helpful as you seek to love and lead those whom the Lord has brought into your life. I hope, more than anything, that it has helped you draw near to the Lord and rejoice in the wisdom that he has given in his Word.

As I have considered my aim in life, I often articulate it to others by saying: My desire is to faithfully and joyfully serve the Lord for my whole life. I say faithfully because I know that many fall away. Be it sin or exhaustion, many quit before the end of the race. I say joyfully because I do not want to serve the Lord or his people begrudgingly. Too many complain about the good work that God has invited us into as his people. These thirty pieces of wisdom have been used by the Lord to help me walk in faithfulness and have served to increase my joy in disciple making. My prayer is that they would serve you in this way also.

In the introduction, I left you with Proverbs 26:7, "Like a lame man's legs, which hang useless, is a proverb in the mouth of fools." This verse reminds us that it is not enough to simply know the truths that we have been discussing. We must, by God's grace, put them into practice.

Notes

1   Newton, Isaac. "Letter from Sir Isaac Newton to Robert Hooke." *Historical Society of Pennsylvania*, 1675.

2   Piper, John. "Seven Lessons for Productivity." *Ask Pastor John* (podcast) July 17, 2020.

3   Smethurst, Matt. Twitter post. October 26, 2020, 3:15 p.m.

4   Spurgeon, Charles. *Lectures to My Students*. Peabody: Hendrickson Publishers, 2010.

LET'S TALK THEOLOGY

Theology matters. Everyone is a theologian because everyone has thoughts about God. The question is, "Are you a good theologian or a bad theologian?" Join Cody on Udemy as he guides listeners through a 4-part series on Systematic Theology.

–

codypodor.com/courses

SYSTEMATIC THEOLOGY

MAY CHRISTIANS SUE?

CODY PODOR

THE CHURCH IS IN NEED OF WISDOM

While many Christians might not pursue litigation, it is very likely that most Christians will encounter litigation on some level.

If Christians are to live faithfully in litigious societies, they must be prepared to respond to matters of law in a biblically informed and theologically comprehensive manner.

–

codypodor.com/may-christians-sue

CPSIA information can be obtained
at www.ICGtesting.com
Printed in the USA
BVHW031645080321
601998BV00007B/876

9 781736 466803